Through Carriage Window

1: Leeds – Settle – Carlisle Circular

by

Len Sims & Chris Darmon

Dalesman Books
1989

The Dalesman Publishing Company Ltd.,
Clapham, via Lancaster, LA2 8EB

First published 1986
Second edition 1989

ISBN: 0 85206 972 3

Printed by Peter Fretwell & Sons Ltd.,
Healey Works, Goulbourne Street, Keighley, West Yorkshire

INTRODUCTION

Journey with us over some of the most beautiful railway routes in Britain, from the industrial landscape of West Yorkshire, to the high Pennine Hills, the majesty of Ribblehead Viaduct, and the historic city of Carlisle. Heading south past lonely Shap and the distant outlines of the high Lakeland Fells, then down to the shores of Morecambe Bay and the University city of Lancaster, and finally eastwards passing close to Ingleton and the beautiful dales village of Clapham to Skipton and back to the starting point at Leeds.

This is a journey with a difference; for the first time there is an easy to follow, page-by-page route map covering every bit of the way. Not only that, but also notes on the history, of the railway and the surrounding places, on the geography, geology and natural history. There's something for one and all - a true travelling companion.

Although the guide has been written starting and finishing at Leeds, it can be used almost as easily joining at any other point on the route. The journey can be completed within a day, and makes a great day out, but for those who wish to explore the area in greater depth there are many places where you can stay, many things to see and do. There are numerous guidebooks to the area, some of which are included in the bibliography.

In preparing this guide, we'd like to thank the members of the Nationwide Geology Club who not only gave us the idea, but also allowed us to try out this novel approach; the Countryside Commision for the encouragement their report *"Interpreting the Heritage of the Settle-Carlisle Railway Line"* gives to such a project; the various District Councils for help with research and permission to use their material; David Joy of the Dalesman Publishing Company for his help and encouragement in bringing about the final book; and finally British Rail for giving us all the opportunity to travel such a spectacular route. Let us hope that such opportunities will not be lost to future generations to gaze "through the carriage window".

Now you've got the book, all you need is the railway ticket, and a great day is in prospect. Then, just sit back and look around you. There's a whole world out there "through the carriage window".

Sheffield, March 1986

Chris Darmon BSc.
Len Sims BSc.

Since the first edition of this book was published there have been a number of developments on the Settle-Carlisle line. On the positive side, a number of stations formerly only open for "Dalesrail" services, have now fully re-opened, thanks to cash help from the local councils en route. The same public bodies have also under-written an increase in the number of train services.

At the time of writing the line has just been pulled back from the brink of total closure by a vast increase in the number of passengers using it. There can be no better time than the present to travel the complete Leeds-Carlisle circuit using "Through the Carriage Window" as your travelling companion.

L.S. & C.J.D.

Sheffield, April 1989

LEEDS — CARLISLE CIRCULAR TOUR

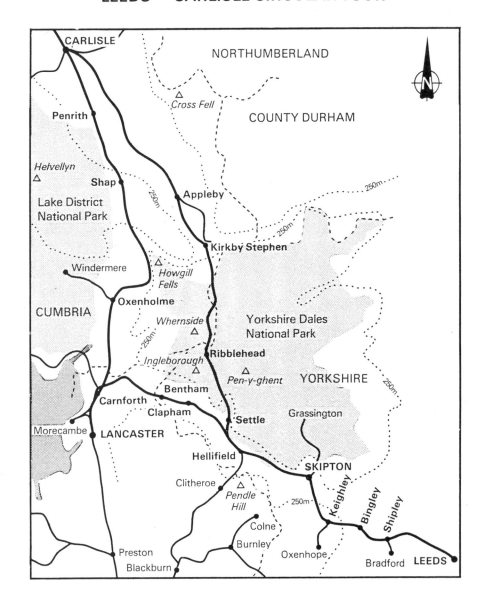

The Natural History of the Route

Leaving the industrial landscape of Leeds behind, rolling sandstone countryside with rich pastures soon takes over - beside the River Aire at Kirkstall Abbey you could be miles from a city. Only the Aire valley towns spoil this rural scene with their pockets of industry and the typical stone mills, Shipley, Bingley and Keighley. Beyond Keighley limestone takes over with a skyline dominated by ancient coral reef structures. Open valleys lined with beech and oak woodlands come into view as gritstones appear towards Hellifield before they are chopped off by the massive South Craven Fault at Settle. Limestone escarpments stretch into the distance both east and west with high craggy limestone country beyond. The mighty power of the earth can most surely be seen to have dramatic effects upon the countryside.

White limestones give way to black slates and grits at Taitlands Tunnel. To the east lies the majestic Pen-y-Ghent (2273ft), seen across the Ribblesdale drumlins, which were deposited as the area lay far beneath the glaciers of the last ice age. North of Horton-in-Ribblesdale, limestone crags and limestone pavements reappear until bleak gritstone moorlands and coniferous forests appear just beyond Ribblehead. Birkett Tunnel marks the beginning of open rolling countryside as firstly limestone and then sandstone appears. These sandstones were deposited in Saharan Desert type conditions some 200 million years ago, and they continue from here to Carlisle.

Southbound from the historic border city of Carlisle the gently rolling country continues as far as Penrith where once again the stark grassy limestone landscape sets in. At Shap the awesome sight of the Shap Granite surrounded by barren moorlands cannot fail to impress. This is land fit only for thinly scattered hill sheep and hardy hill farmers. The outlook does not change for some miles as slates and grits continue almost without interruption until Oxenholme; whilst to the east, the high peaks of the Lake District can be seen against the skyline. At Oxenholme, the familiar limestone reappears and continues southwards following the route as its skirts Morecambe Bay and on into the ancient City of Lancaster.

Heading northwards again from Lancaster back to Leeds via Carnforth the gentle limestone pastures and small stands of trees give way to more rolling and wooded gritstone scenery around Arkenholme. Beyond Bentham, with the Craven Fault scarp rapidly approaching, views of Ingleborough, and on a clear day, Pen-y-Ghent appear as the train rejoins the outward route at Settle Junction and heads south to Leeds.

Settlement Along the Route

To the casual observer, the entire route is Northern England, true, but such a description belittles the differences between Yorkshire, Cumbria and Lancashire. Nowewhere is the relationship between the land, man and his home and work more clearly seen than by observing the pattern of towns and villages along the route.

Leeds, the bustling self-styled "capital of Northern England" has a surprisingly long history, with monks from the nearby Kirkstall Abbey living in the lush valley of the River Aire as early as 1152. The modern city, however, is a product of the nineteenth century, grown wealthy on textiles and engineering. Today, it is the third largest city in England, with many fine buildings, parks and institutions.

The mill towns of the Aire Valley, Shipley, Bingley and Keighley seem to vie with each other as to who could have the finest mill building or the tallest chimney. Sadly these monoliths to the Victorian age are now all too often half empty and falling down, the woollen industry they served having declined dramatically in recent years; but what fine buildings they have left us. Even the houses, built from the local robust sandstones are often as good as the day they were built. Just past Shipley is the world famous mill village of Saltaire, a complete community, conceived and built by just one man, mill owner Titus Salt - a northern model village in the same vein as Cadbury's Bournville, near Birmingham.

Beyond Keighley, with the youthful River Aire, the mills and their communities are much smaller. This is sheep and cattle country, with small villages, now more likely filled with city folk making the daily journey to work further down the Aire Valley. Skipton marks the gateway to the Yorkshire Dales, with its ancient castle and bustling markets. Historically the town has guarded the Aire Gap, separating the Northern and Southern Pennines, putting the town on a variety of important routes by road, rail and canal. Today, Skipton is a market town for dales folk, which doubles as a thriving tourist centre, offering food and accommodation for the many visitors who throng its streets during the summer months.

Hellifield is the first of several settlements where the coming of the railway has had a marked effect. The large station is evidence that this was once a busy junction. The rows of Midland Railway houses show how many were once employed. Settle, marks the start of the upland area, nestling below the limestone crags formed by the great Craven Faults. The little town has services well beyond its size; with a variety of hotels, restaurants and cafes to suit any pocket. Market day is Tuesday, and is something not to be missed, with craven folk still bringing their produce to sell.

North of Settle, and with every mile of climb, the settlements seem to become smaller, Horton-in-Ribblesdale, Ribblehead, Dent and Garsdale. Even the farms are few and far between in this wild, forbidding country. Close to the railway, the occasional railwayman's cottage, marks the influence this one main line had. Kirkby Stephen is an interesting and historic small market town and centre for exploring the Upper Eden Valley. Historic Appleby, former county town of Westmorland, is set amidst the rolling pastoral landscape of the Eden Valley. The town is famous for its annual gypsy horse fair, held in early June, which attracts visitors from all over the country.

Carlisle, the border city, goes back over 2,000 years to the Celts, and certainly the Romans appreciated how important the place was, marking as it did, the western end of Hadrian's Wall. Even the station, dating from 1876, seems to announce the importance of the city. There's certainly plenty to see and do here, with castle, cathedral, market and modern shopping centre, and if you've time, plenty of recreational facilities.

Penrith marks one of the gateways to the Lake District, popular with tourists throughout the year. It's an ancient market town, dominated by the ruined castle. The local sandstone, quarried from the hill just above the town, makes splendid red buildings. Heading south, lonely Shap is a community which has been built on granite quarrying. Watch out for Tebay, one of the saddest spectacles. The rows of terraced houses, many of which stand empty, are all that remains of a once thriving community. This place died one day in 1968 with the closure of the engine sheds, as steam was displaced, first by diesel and then electric. Tebay epitomises the railway town - take away the railway and it dies.

Just north of Oxenholme and slightly to the west of the line, is the thriving lakeland town of Kendal, which manages to combine industry with tourism, and does both well. The result is a lively, bustling place offering excellent facilities. With the appearance of good agricultural country, comes small villages and large farms, which take us almost to the edge of Morecambe Bay. Carnforth is yet another railway community, but one which has faired better than others. Even the former engine shed and yard is busy - echoing to the sound of steam engines at the Steamtown Museum.

As we skirt around Morecambe Bay it's but a short distance to the pleasure beaches of such resorts as Morecambe and Heysham. Alighting from the train at Lancaster, the mock tudor station belies the genuine historic nature of this fine University City. Lancaster is a town which seems to be full of museums and monuments - don't miss it.

Heading eastwards from Carnforth the lush pastures seem to have encouraged the growth of solid looking villages with equally solid, square farmhouses. Only Bentham with its corn mills and factories intrudes into the otherwise idyllic scene. Clapham village, some way from the station, is one of the most beautiful villages in the dales, set at the edge of the limestone country with its famous caves and potholes. Beyond Giggleswick, famous for its public school, lies Settle Junction and the rejoining of our outward journey.

Railway History of the Route

With the railways of Britain nationalised since 1948 and now one of our most under-used assets, it's hard to imagine the rivalries that existed between the various railway companies, to build the nineteenth century 'iron road'. As the brief notes below show, there's plenty of history in the making of our railway route.

Leeds - Skipton
The present Leeds (City) became the only major station with the closure of Central in 1967. The present structure dates from then. The line to Shipley formed part of the Leeds-Bradford line built in 1846, with the Shipley-Skipton section completed in 1847. Both parts were operated by the Midland Railway until 1923, and then the LMS until 1948.

Skipton-Clapham/ Lancaster (Green Ayre)
This line formed part of the London & North Western Railway and was built in 1849/50. The main line in fact continued beyond Clapham to Ingleton.

Settle-Carlisle
The Midland Railway opened the magnificent Settle-Carlisle railway in 1876, the entire 72 miles having been completed in 6 years, involving up to 6,000 navvies and costing nearly £3.5 million. It was built to give the Midland trains their own route to Scotland, but it was overtaken by events, and in fact was the railway no-one wanted. As you speed across one of the viaducts or flash through one of the tunnels, remember this line was built without the aid of mechanical shovels - just shear blood, sweat and toil.

Carlisle-Lancaster
The whole 70 miles of this railway was built in less than 2 ½ years, at a cost of just £1.2 million. It opened for traffic in 1848 and very soon became a major part of the West Coast route of the LNWR from London-Scotland; a task it still performs today. The building wasn't without incident however, with major riots amongst the navvies at Penrith!

Carnforth-Wennington
This stretch of line, built jointly by the Midland and the Furness companies and opened in 1867, only assumed importance after 1966 with the closure of the direct route between Wennington and Lancaster (Green Ayre). It's an odd fact that railway "progress" in recent years, has often led to long detours!

For greater detail of the railway history, readers are referred to the bibliography at the back of this book, where a number of popular titles are listed.

KEY TO THE MAP PAGES

station open for passengers	■
station closed	□
hill with height	△
lineside building	◆
Youth Hostel	▲

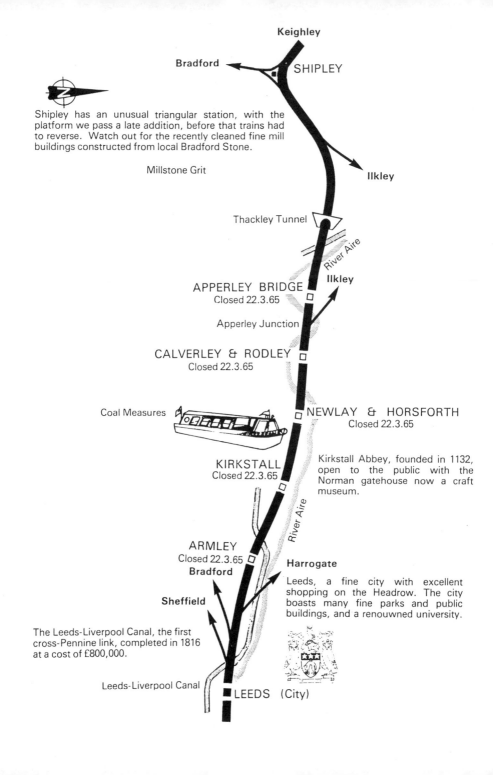

Keighley

Bradford ◄— **SHIPLEY**

Shipley has an unusual triangular station, with the platform we pass a late addition, before that trains had to reverse. Watch out for the recently cleaned fine mill buildings constructed from local Bradford Stone.

Millstone Grit

Ilkley

Thackley Tunnel

River Aire

Ilkley

APPERLEY BRIDGE
Closed 22.3.65

Apperley Junction

CALVERLEY & RODLEY
Closed 22.3.65

Coal Measures

NEWLAY & HORSFORTH
Closed 22.3.65

KIRKSTALL
Closed 22.3.65

Kirkstall Abbey, founded in 1132, open to the public with the Norman gatehouse now a craft museum.

River Aire

ARMLEY
Closed 22.3.65
Bradford

Harrogate

Sheffield

Leeds, a fine city with excellent shopping on the Headrow. The city boasts many fine parks and public buildings, and a renouwned university.

The Leeds-Liverpool Canal, the first cross-Pennine link, completed in 1816 at a cost of £800,000.

Leeds-Liverpool Canal

■■ **LEEDS** (City)

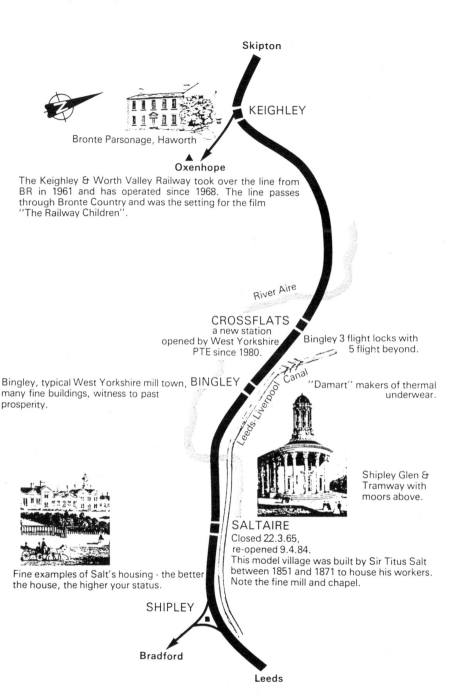

Skipton

KEIGHLEY

Bronte Parsonage, Haworth

Oxenhope

The Keighley & Worth Valley Railway took over the line from BR in 1961 and has operated since 1968. The line passes through Bronte Country and was the setting for the film "The Railway Children".

River Aire

CROSSFLATS
a new station
opened by West Yorkshire
PTE since 1980.

Bingley 3 flight locks with 5 flight beyond.

Bingley, typical West Yorkshire mill town, BINGLEY many fine buildings, witness to past prosperity.

Leeds-Liverpool Canal

"Damart" makers of thermal underwear.

Shipley Glen & Tramway with moors above.

SALTAIRE
Closed 22.3.65,
re-opened 9.4.84.
This model village was built by Sir Titus Salt between 1851 and 1871 to house his workers. Note the fine mill and chapel.

Fine examples of Salt's housing - the better the house, the higher your status.

SHIPLEY

Bradford

Leeds

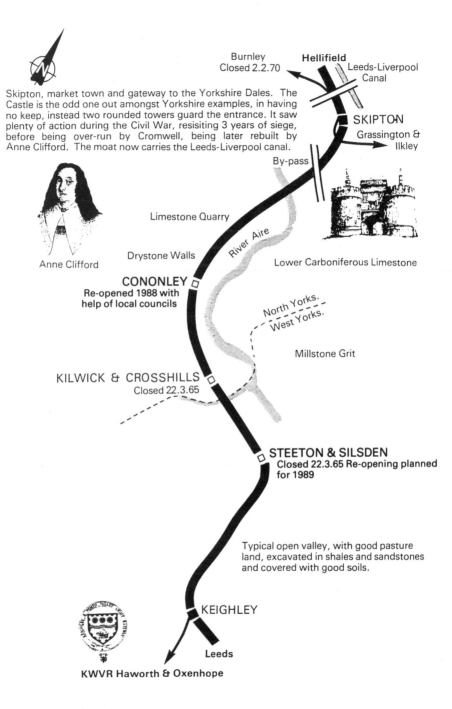

Burnley
Closed 2.2.70

Hellifield

Leeds-Liverpool
Canal

Skipton, market town and gateway to the Yorkshire Dales. The Castle is the odd one out amongst Yorkshire examples, in having no keep, instead two rounded towers guard the entrance. It saw plenty of action during the Civil War, resisiting 3 years of siege, before being over-run by Cromwell, being later rebuilt by Anne Clifford. The moat now carries the Leeds-Liverpool canal.

SKIPTON

Grassington &
Ilkley

By-pass

Limestone Quarry

River Aire

Drystone Walls

Anne Clifford

Lower Carboniferous Limestone

CONONLEY
**Re-opened 1988 with
help of local councils**

North Yorks.
West Yorks.

Millstone Grit

KILWICK & CROSSHILLS
Closed 22.3.65

STEETON & SILSDEN
**Closed 22.3.65 Re-opening planned
for 1989**

Typical open valley, with good pasture land, excavated in shales and sandstones and covered with good soils.

KEIGHLEY

Leeds

KWVR Haworth & Oxenhope

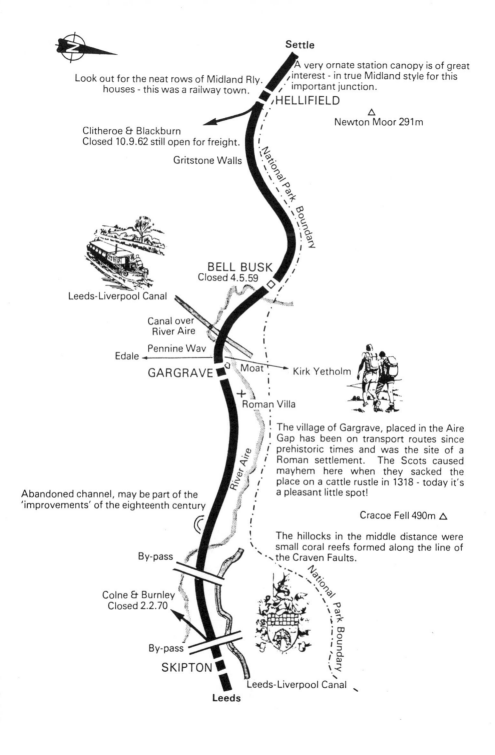

Settle

Look out for the neat rows of Midland Rly. houses - this was a railway town.

A very ornate station canopy is of great interest - in true Midland style for this important junction.

HELLIFIELD

△
Newton Moor 291m

Clitheroe & Blackburn
Closed 10.9.62 still open for freight.

Gritstone Walls

National Park Boundary

Leeds-Liverpool Canal

BELL BUSK
Closed 4.5.59

Canal over
River Aire

Pennine Way

Edale ←

GARGRAVE ← Moat → Kirk Yetholm

+
Roman Villa

The village of Gargrave, placed in the Aire Gap has been on transport routes since prehistoric times and was the site of a Roman settlement. The Scots caused mayhem here when they sacked the place on a cattle rustle in 1318 - today it's a pleasant little spot!

River Aire

Abandoned channel, may be part of the 'improvements' of the eighteenth century

Cracoe Fell 490m △

The hillocks in the middle distance were small coral reefs formed along the line of the Craven Faults.

By-pass

Colne & Burnley
Closed 2.2.70

National Park Boundary

By-pass

SKIPTON

Leeds-Liverpool Canal

Leeds

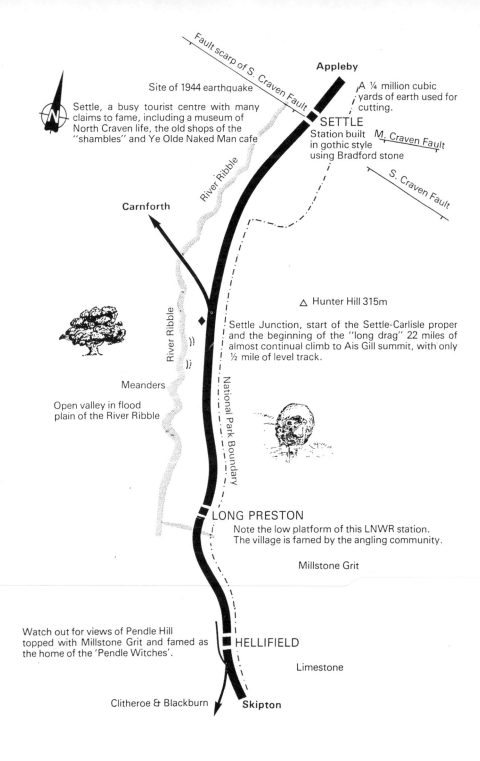

Fault scarp of S. Craven Fault

Appleby

Site of 1944 earthquake

A ¼ million cubic yards of earth used for cutting.

Settle, a busy tourist centre with many claims to fame, including a museum of North Craven life, the old shops of the "shambles" and Ye Olde Naked Man cafe

SETTLE

Station built in gothic style using Bradford stone

M. Craven Fault

S. Craven Fault

River Ribble

Carnforth

△ Hunter Hill 315m

River Ribble

Settle Junction, start of the Settle-Carlisle proper and the beginning of the "long drag" 22 miles of almost continual climb to Ais Gill summit, with only ½ mile of level track.

Meanders

Open valley in flood plain of the River Ribble

National Park Boundary

LONG PRESTON

Note the low platform of this LNWR station. The village is famed by the angling community.

Millstone Grit

Watch out for views of Pendle Hill topped with Millstone Grit and famed as the home of the 'Pendle Witches'.

HELLIFIELD

Limestone

Clitheroe & Blackburn

Skipton

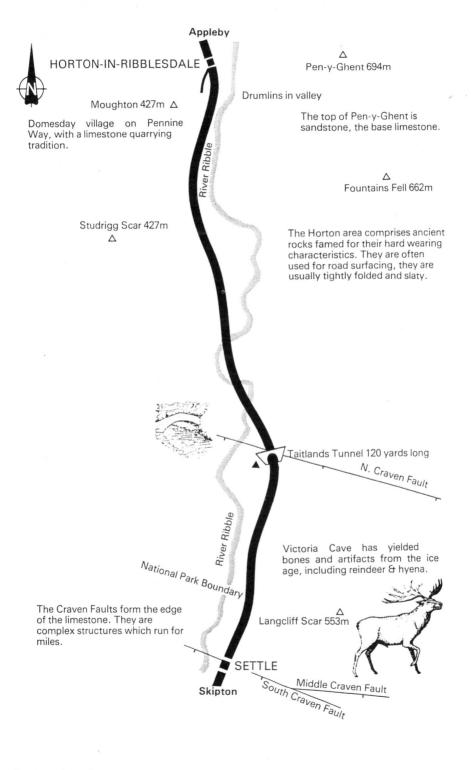

Appleby

HORTON-IN-RIBBLESDALE

△
Pen-y-Ghent 694m

Moughton 427m △

Drumlins in valley

Domesday village on Pennine Way, with a limestone quarrying tradition.

The top of Pen-y-Ghent is sandstone, the base limestone.

River Ribble

△
Fountains Fell 662m

Studrigg Scar 427m
△

The Horton area comprises ancient rocks famed for their hard wearing characteristics. They are often used for road surfacing, they are usually tightly folded and slaty.

Taitlands Tunnel 120 yards long

N. Craven Fault

River Ribble

National Park Boundary

Victoria Cave has yielded bones and artifacts from the ice age, including reindeer & hyena.

The Craven Faults form the edge of the limestone. They are complex structures which run for miles.

Langcliff Scar 553m △

SETTLE

Skipton

Middle Craven Fault

South Craven Fault

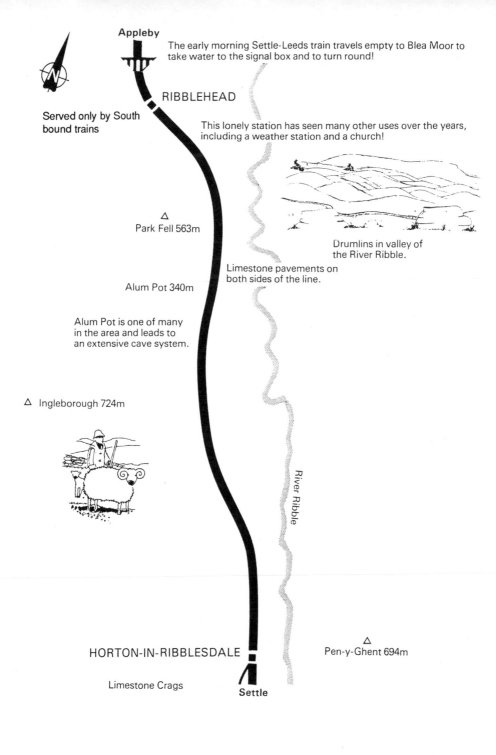

Appleby

The early morning Settle-Leeds train travels empty to Blea Moor to take water to the signal box and to turn round!

RIBBLEHEAD

Served only by South bound trains

This lonely station has seen many other uses over the years, including a weather station and a church!

△
Park Fell 563m

Drumlins in valley of the River Ribble.

Limestone pavements on both sides of the line.

Alum Pot 340m

Alum Pot is one of many in the area and leads to an extensive cave system.

△ Ingleborough 724m

River Ribble

HORTON-IN-RIBBLESDALE

△
Pen-y-Ghent 694m

Limestone Crags

Settle

Appleby

Plantation

DENT

At a height of 1,100ft the station is the highest on an English main line. The access road rises at 20% from the village.

In 1963 snowdrifts were over 20ft deep here, the remains of old snow fences can be seen beside the line. House Martins, under the station eaves are reputed to be amongst the highest of their breed.

Arten Gill Viaduct 11 arches, 660ft long 117ft high in Dent "marble"

△
Great Knoutberry
Hill 672m

Dent, birthplace of Adam Sedgwick in 1785. A pioneer geologist, he is commemorated by a Shap Granite boulder in the village. The village is still cobbled and retains much of the character of the dales. Worth a visit.

Dent Head Viaduct 10 arches, 596ft long and 110ft high of local 'blue' limestone.

Coal seam

This project cost £45 per yard and terrible conditions were encountered in its construction. A system of tramways on the hill brought materials to the ventilations shafts for work below. Gritstone together with locally made bricks and mortar were all needed. Less than a dozen serious injuries were reported, despite the reputation for its being haunted!

Cumbria
N. Yorks.

Blea Moor Tunnel 2629 yards

△
Blea Moor 535m

Gritstone

△
Whernside 736m

Dales Way

Little Dale

Rusty water in stream.

Lonely Blea Moor signal box, still manned.
Ribblehead Viaduct, 24 arches, 440yards long, 100ft high, symbol of the Settle-Carlisle railway. The piers are set deep in Batty Moss, and the whole structure is buttressed with massive embankments. Despite being well built of limestone the problem now is that the whole structure is crumbling away from the inside.

At St. Leonard's church in Chapel-le-Dale is a monument to over 100 men who died in the construction of the railway.

RIBBLEHEAD
Served only by South
bound trains

Settle

Limestone

Appleby

River Eden

Nat. Park Boundary

Watershed - North flow to River Eden, South to River Ure.

Ais Gill summit 1169ft. The signalbox and community now gone, the former for preservation in Derbyshire.

Cumbria
N. Yorks.

△ Abbotside Common 666m

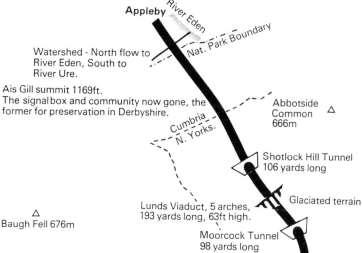

△ Shotlock Hill Tunnel 106 yards long

Glaciated terrain

Lunds Viaduct, 5 arches, 193 yards long, 63ft high.

△ Baugh Fell 676m

△ Moorcock Tunnel 98 yards long

Dandry Mire Viaduct, 12 arches, 227 yards long 50ft high, should have been a bank, but the bog kept swallowing up the material tipped into it - note the wide embankments on either side of the viaduct.

GARSDALE

Hawes & Northallerton Closed 16.3.59

Garsdale, the only true junction on the line, lies at the entrance to Wensleydale. Here were the highest water troughs in the world, supplied with water from a large tank underneath which was a room which was for a time the local meeting room and library. The turntable had to be stockaded to stop engines being blown off!

Plantation of conifers

Rise Hill Tunnel - 1213 yards long was driven through wet, unstable rocks. There are two air shafts to the moor above.

△ Rise Hill 556m

△ Widdale Fell 586m

DENT

Old Coal Road to Dent village 2½ miles.

Settle

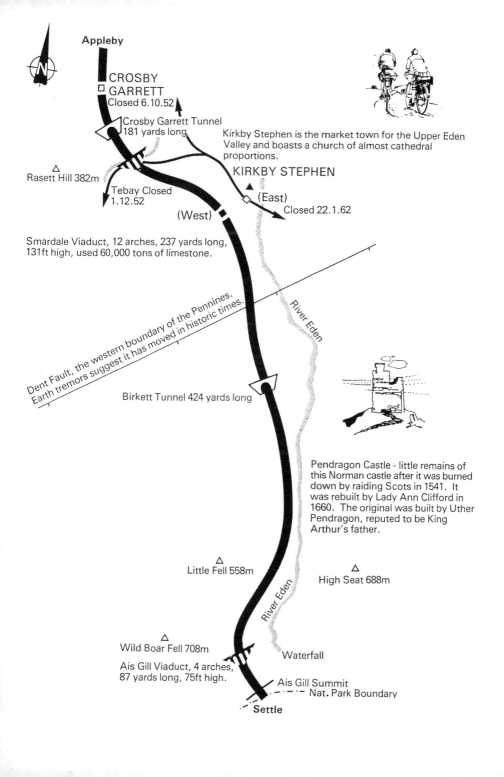

Appleby

CROSBY
GARRETT
Closed 6.10.52

Crosby Garrett Tunnel
181 yards long

Kirkby Stephen is the market town for the Upper Eden
Valley and boasts a church of almost cathedral
proportions.

△
Rasett Hill 382m

KIRKBY STEPHEN

Tebay Closed
1.12.52

▲ (East)

(West)

Closed 22.1.62

Smardale Viaduct, 12 arches, 237 yards long,
131ft high, used 60,000 tons of limestone.

Dent Fault, the western boundary of the Pennines.
Earth tremors suggest it has moved in historic times.

River Eden

Birkett Tunnel 424 yards long

Pendragon Castle - little remains of
this Norman castle after it was burned
down by raiding Scots in 1541. It
was rebuilt by Lady Ann Clifford in
1660. The original was built by Uther
Pendragon, reputed to be King
Arthur's father.

△
Little Fell 558m

△
High Seat 688m

River Eden

△
Wild Boar Fell 708m

Ais Gill Viaduct, 4 arches,
87 yards long, 75ft high.

Waterfall

Ais Gill Summit
Nat. Park Boundary

Settle

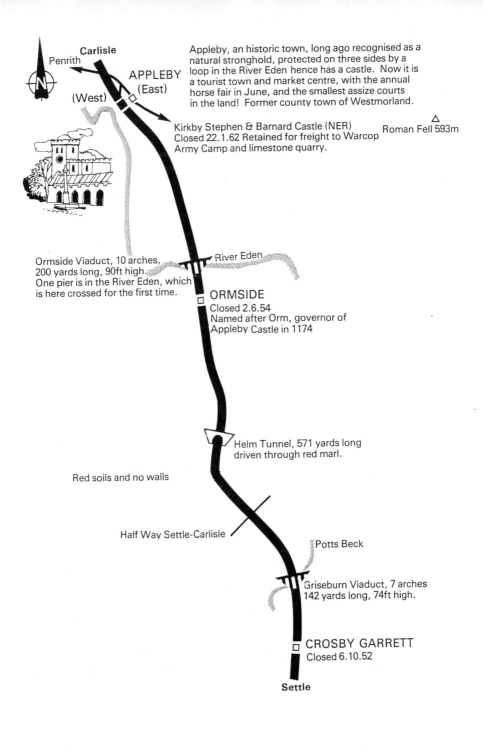

Carlisle
Penrith
APPLEBY (East)
(West)

Appleby, an historic town, long ago recognised as a natural stronghold, protected on three sides by a loop in the River Eden hence has a castle. Now it is a tourist town and market centre, with the annual horse fair in June, and the smallest assize courts in the land! Former county town of Westmorland.

Roman Fell 593m

Kirkby Stephen & Barnard Castle (NER) Closed 22.1.62 Retained for freight to Warcop Army Camp and limestone quarry.

Ormside Viaduct, 10 arches, 200 yards long, 90ft high. One pier is in the River Eden, which is here crossed for the first time.

River Eden

ORMSIDE
Closed 2.6.54
Named after Orm, governor of Appleby Castle in 1174

Helm Tunnel, 571 yards long driven through red marl.

Red soils and no walls

Half Way Settle-Carlisle

Potts Beck

Griseburn Viaduct, 7 arches 142 yards long, 74ft high.

CROSBY GARRETT
Closed 6.10.52

Settle

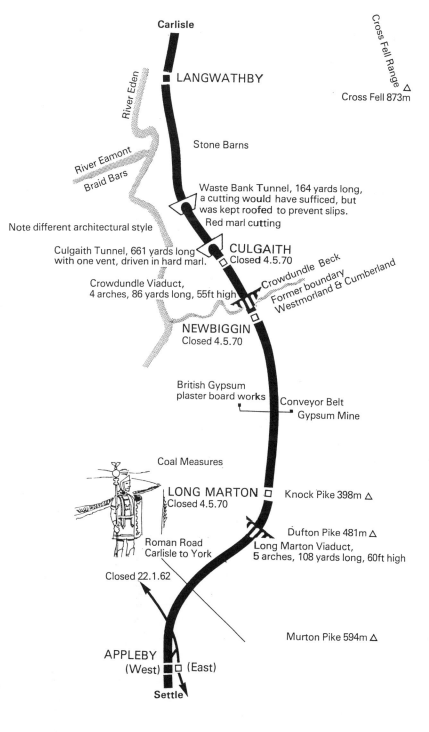

Carlisle

Cross Fell Range

LANGWATHBY

Cross Fell 873m △

River Eden

Stone Barns

River Eamont

Braid Bars

Waste Bank Tunnel, 164 yards long,
a cutting would have sufficed, but
was kept roofed to prevent slips.

Red marl cutting

Note different architectural style

Culgaith Tunnel, 661 yards long,
with one vent, driven in hard marl.

CULGAITH
Closed 4.5.70

Crowdundle Beck

Crowdundle Viaduct,
4 arches, 86 yards long, 55ft high

Former boundary
Westmorland & Cumberland

NEWBIGGIN
Closed 4.5.70

British Gypsum
plaster board works

Conveyor Belt

Gypsum Mine

Coal Measures

LONG MARTON
Closed 4.5.70

Knock Pike 398m △

Dufton Pike 481m △

Roman Road
Carlisle to York

Long Marton Viaduct,
5 arches, 108 yards long, 60ft high

Closed 22.1.62

Murton Pike 594m △

APPLEBY
(West) □ (East)

Settle

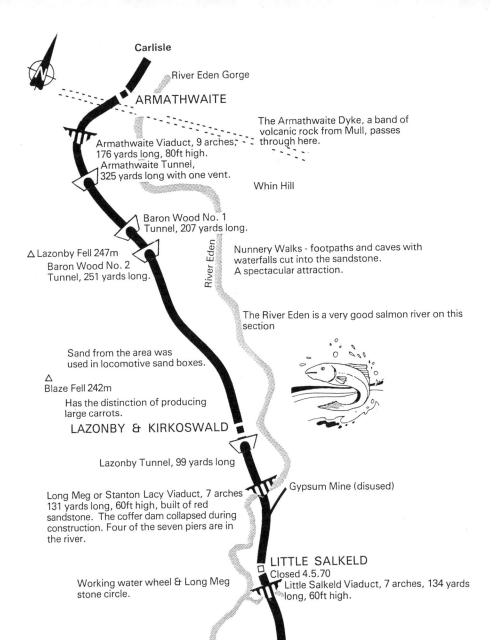

Carlisle

River Eden Gorge

ARMATHWAITE

The Armathwaite Dyke, a band of volcanic rock from Mull, passes through here.

Armathwaite Viaduct, 9 arches, 176 yards long, 80ft high.
Armathwaite Tunnel, 325 yards long with one vent.

Whin Hill

Baron Wood No. 1 Tunnel, 207 yards long.

△ Lazonby Fell 247m
Baron Wood No. 2 Tunnel, 251 yards long.

Nunnery Walks - footpaths and caves with waterfalls cut into the sandstone. A spectacular attraction.

River Eden

The River Eden is a very good salmon river on this section

Sand from the area was used in locomotive sand boxes.

△ Blaze Fell 242m

Has the distinction of producing large carrots.

LAZONBY & KIRKOSWALD

Lazonby Tunnel, 99 yards long

Long Meg or Stanton Lacy Viaduct, 7 arches 131 yards long, 60ft high, built of red sandstone. The coffer dam collapsed during construction. Four of the seven piers are in the river.

Gypsum Mine (disused)

Working water wheel & Long Meg stone circle.

LITTLE SALKELD
Closed 4.5.70
Little Salkeld Viaduct, 7 arches, 134 yards long, 60ft high.

LANGWATHBY

Appleby

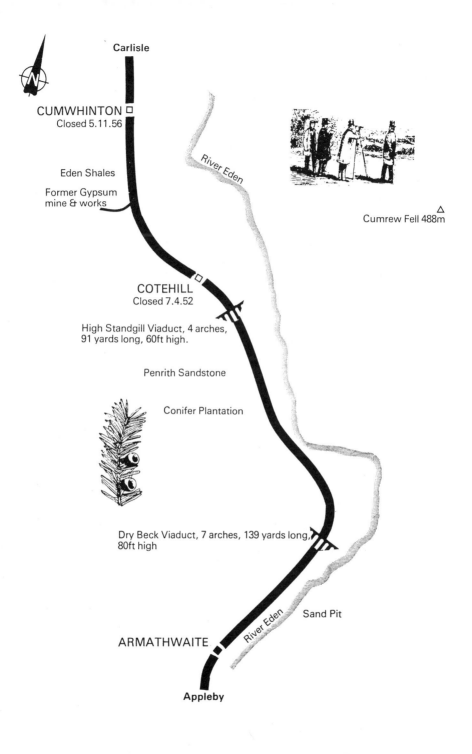

Carlisle

CUMWHINTON ▯
Closed 5.11.56

River Eden

Eden Shales

Former Gypsum
mine & works

△
Cumrew Fell 488m

COTEHILL ▯
Closed 7.4.52

High Standgill Viaduct, 4 arches,
91 yards long, 60ft high.

Penrith Sandstone

Conifer Plantation

Dry Beck Viaduct, 7 arches, 139 yards long,
80ft high

Sand Pit

ARMATHWAITE   River Eden

Appleby

Scotland

River Eden

Carlisle, the ancient border city. is situated at the confluence of the Rivers Caldew and Eden. The city boasts a fine cathedral and castle. The city remained unconquered for 26 years after 1066. The massive keep of the castle remains to this day. You will also find a fine market and modern shopping mall 'The Lanes'. There are plenty of reminders of past wealth in the many stone buildings. The City Trail is well worth following.

Solway Firth

River Caldew

Silloth Closed 7.9.64

Castle

The Carlisle avoiding line, closed and lifted following a freight train derailment at River Caldew bridge

Cathedral

CARLISLE

Citadel Station, a mere fraction of its former glory, represented co-operation between 8 railway companies. all of whom used it prior to 1923. Each company had its own goods facilities, yards and engine shed.

The Newcastle-Carlisle railway opened as early as May 1st. 1839.

Newcastle

SCOTBY
Closed 1.2.42

Whitehaven & Barrow

Penrith

St. Bees Sandstone

CUMWHINTON
Closed 5.11.56

Appleby

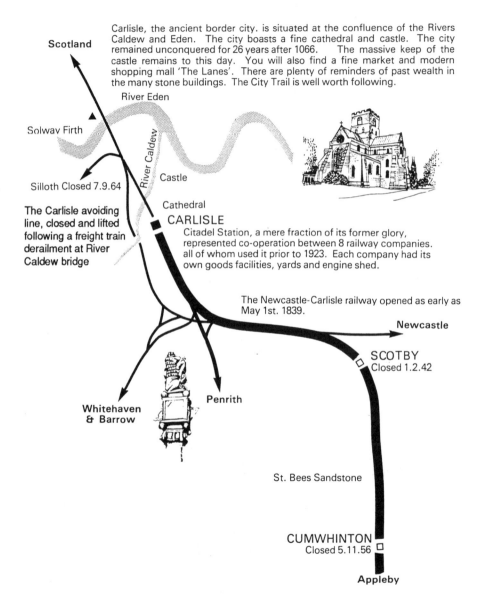

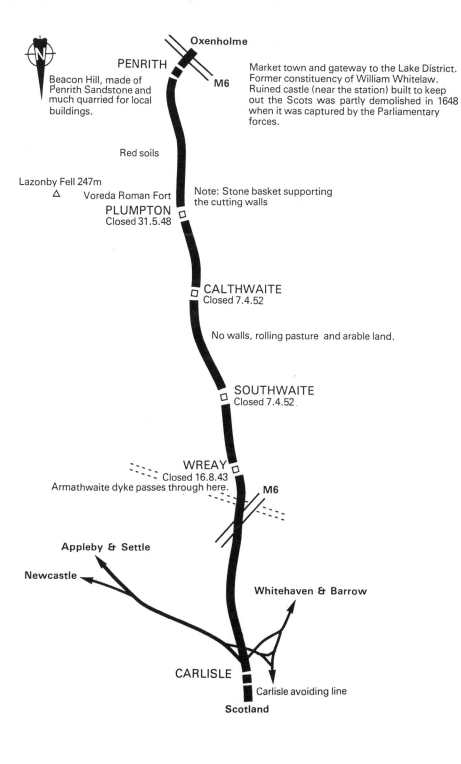

N

Oxenholme

PENRITH

Beacon Hill, made of Penrith Sandstone and much quarried for local buildings.

M6

Market town and gateway to the Lake District. Former constituency of William Whitelaw. Ruined castle (near the station) built to keep out the Scots was partly demolished in 1648 when it was captured by the Parliamentary forces.

Red soils

Lazonby Fell 247m
△   Voreda Roman Fort

Note: Stone basket supporting the cutting walls

PLUMPTON
Closed 31.5.48

CALTHWAITE
Closed 7.4.52

No walls, rolling pasture and arable land.

SOUTHWAITE
Closed 7.4.52

WREAY
Closed 16.8.43
Armathwaite dyke passes through here.

M6

Appleby & Settle

Newcastle

Whitehaven & Barrow

CARLISLE

Carlisle avoiding line

Scotland

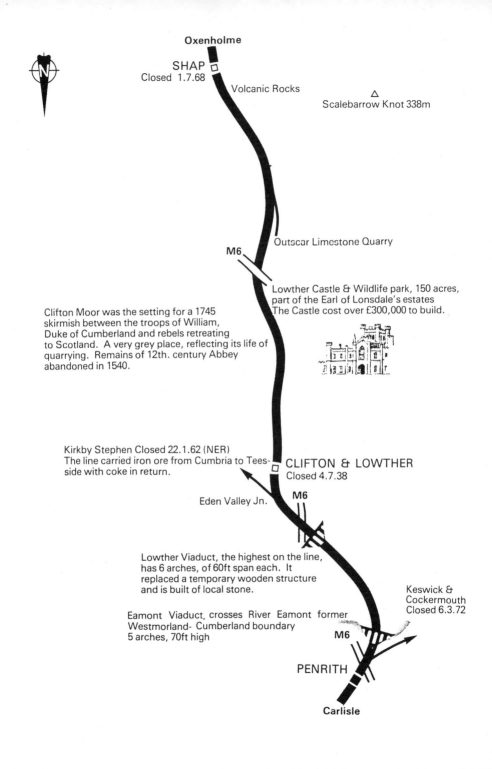

Oxenholme

SHAP
Closed 1.7.68

Volcanic Rocks

△
Scalebarrow Knot 338m

Outscar Limestone Quarry

M6

Lowther Castle & Wildlife park, 150 acres,
part of the Earl of Lonsdale's estates
The Castle cost over £300,000 to build.

Clifton Moor was the setting for a 1745
skirmish between the troops of William,
Duke of Cumberland and rebels retreating
to Scotland. A very grey place, reflecting its life of
quarrying. Remains of 12th. century Abbey
abandoned in 1540.

Kirkby Stephen Closed 22.1.62 (NER)
The line carried iron ore from Cumbria to Tees-
side with coke in return.

CLIFTON & LOWTHER
Closed 4.7.38

Eden Valley Jn.

M6

Lowther Viaduct, the highest on the line,
has 6 arches, of 60ft span each. It
replaced a temporary wooden structure
and is built of local stone.

Keswick &
Cockermouth
Closed 6.3.72

Eamont Viaduct, crosses River Eamont former
Westmorland- Cumberland boundary
5 arches, 70ft high

M6

PENRITH

Carlisle

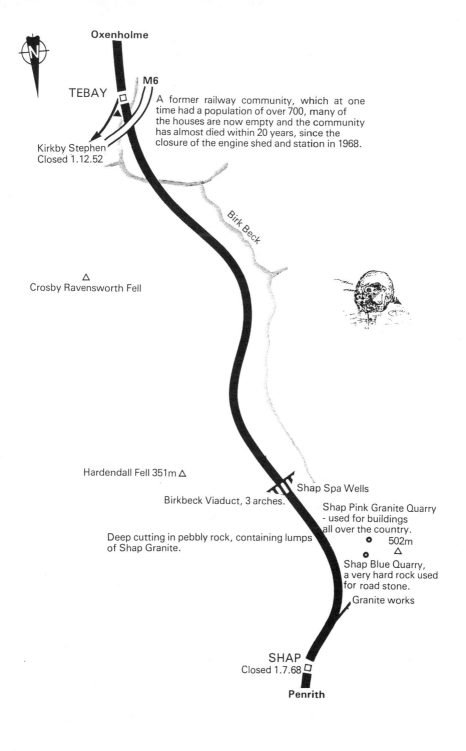

Oxenholme

N

M6

TEBAY

A former railway community, which at one time had a population of over 700, many of the houses are now empty and the community has almost died within 20 years, since the closure of the engine shed and station in 1968.

Kirkby Stephen
Closed 1.12.52

Birk Beck

△
Crosby Ravensworth Fell

Hardendall Fell 351m △

Shap Spa Wells

Birkbeck Viaduct, 3 arches.

Shap Pink Granite Quarry - used for buildings all over the country.

Deep cutting in pebbly rock, containing lumps of Shap Granite.

o   502m
o   △

Shap Blue Quarry, a very hard rock used for road stone.

Granite works

SHAP
Closed 1.7.68

Penrith

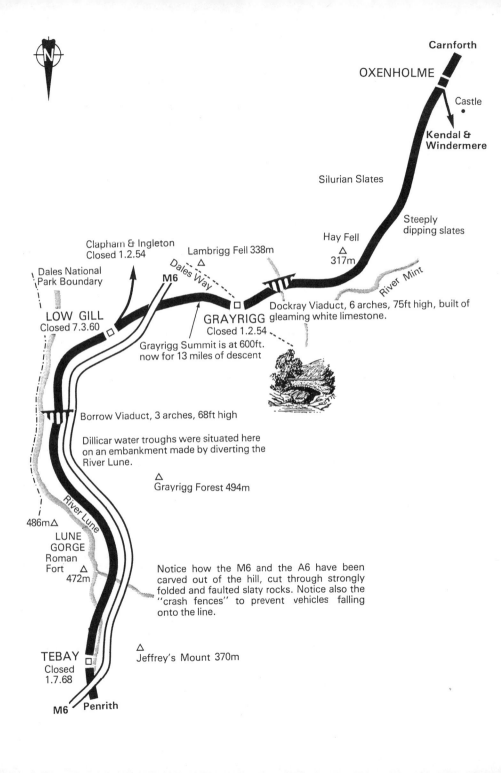

Carnforth

OXENHOLME

Castle

Kendal &
Windermere

Silurian Slates

Steeply
dipping slates

Clapham & Ingleton
Closed 1.2.54

Lambrigg Fell 338m

Hay Fell
△
317m

Dales Way

M6

River Mint

Dales National
Park Boundary

LOW GILL
Closed 7.3.60

GRAYRIGG
Closed 1.2.54

Dockray Viaduct, 6 arches, 75ft high, built of
gleaming white limestone.

Grayrigg Summit is at 600ft.
now for 13 miles of descent

Borrow Viaduct, 3 arches, 68ft high

Dillicar water troughs were situated here
on an embankment made by diverting the
River Lune.

△
Grayrigg Forest 494m

River Lune

486m △

LUNE
GORGE
Roman
Fort   △
         472m

Notice how the M6 and the A6 have been
carved out of the hill, cut through strongly
folded and faulted slaty rocks. Notice also the
"crash fences" to prevent vehicles falling
onto the line.

△
Jeffrey's Mount 370m

TEBAY
Closed
1.7.68

M6   Penrith

Lancaster

Settle Jn.

◇ **CARNFORTH**
Steamtown in the old yard and shed area, note the coaling stage.

Carnforth, Oxenholme, Tebay and Penrith were long regarded as being amongst the draughtiest, darkest and ugliest stations in England!

Barrow in Furness

△ **Warton Crag 163m**

Lancaster Canal - this section went to Kendal and was opened in 1819 and closed at this point in 1955. Restoration would not be possible without a tunnel under the A76.

● Leighton Hall, built of gleaming limestone.

BURTON & HOLME
Closed 27.3.50

△
Hutton Roof Crags 274m

2 arched limestone bridge across River Beela.

At nearby Endmoor, gunpowder was made in the 1940s and brought to the railway by horse and cart, there were reports of several fatal explosions.

HM Prison

△
Farlton Fell 244m

MILNTHORPE
Closed 1.7.68

Arnside
Closed 1.3.53

Deer Park 95m △

Levens Hall, a tudor mansion

Watch out for the overgrown Lancaster Canal which passes under the railway in a 378 yard tunnel which consumed 3 million bricks when it was built. Hincaster Junction

△
The Helm 185m

OXENHOME

**Kendal &
Winderemere**

Penrith

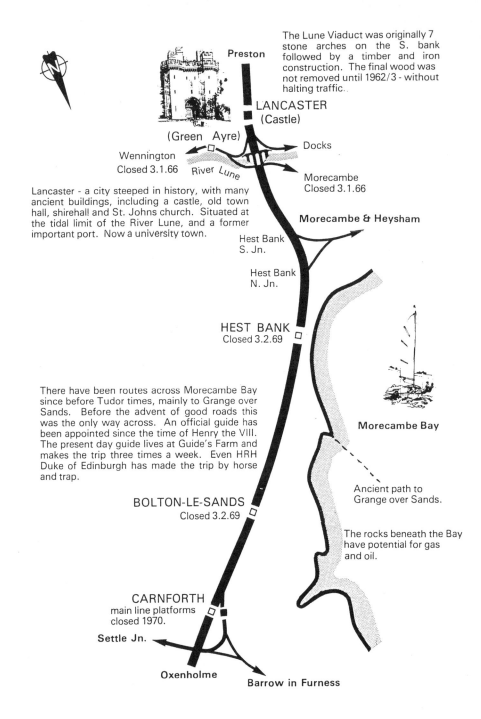

Preston

The Lune Viaduct was originally 7 stone arches on the S. bank followed by a timber and iron construction. The final wood was not removed until 1962/3 - without halting traffic.

LANCASTER
(Castle)

(Green Ayre)

Docks

Wennington
Closed 3.1.66

River Lune

Morecambe
Closed 3.1.66

Lancaster - a city steeped in history, with many ancient buildings, including a castle, old town hall, shirehall and St. Johns church. Situated at the tidal limit of the River Lune, and a former important port. Now a university town.

Morecambe & Heysham

Hest Bank
S. Jn.

Hest Bank
N. Jn.

HEST BANK
Closed 3.2.69

There have been routes across Morecambe Bay since before Tudor times, mainly to Grange over Sands. Before the advent of good roads this was the only way across. An official guide has been appointed since the time of Henry the VIII. The present day guide lives at Guide's Farm and makes the trip three times a week. Even HRH Duke of Edinburgh has made the trip by horse and trap.

Morecambe Bay

Ancient path to Grange over Sands.

BOLTON-LE-SANDS
Closed 3.2.69

The rocks beneath the Bay have potential for gas and oil.

CARNFORTH
main line platforms
closed 1970.

Settle Jn.

Oxenholme

Barrow in Furness

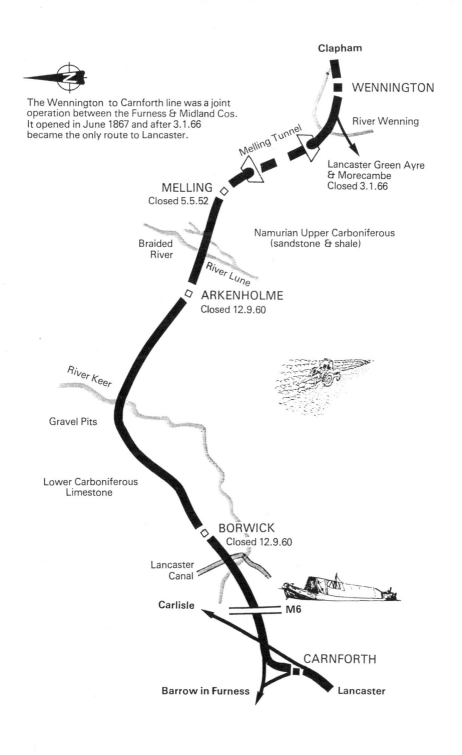

Clapham

WENNINGTON

The Wennington to Carnforth line was a joint operation between the Furness & Midland Cos. It opened in June 1867 and after 3.1.66 became the only route to Lancaster.

Melling Tunnel

River Wenning

Lancaster Green Ayre
& Morecambe
Closed 3.1.66

MELLING
Closed 5.5.52

Namurian Upper Carboniferous
(sandstone & shale)

Braided
River

River Lune

ARKENHOLME
Closed 12.9.60

River Keer

Gravel Pits

Lower Carboniferous
Limestone

BORWICK
Closed 12.9.60

Lancaster
Canal

Carlisle

M6

CARNFORTH

Barrow in Furness

Lancaster

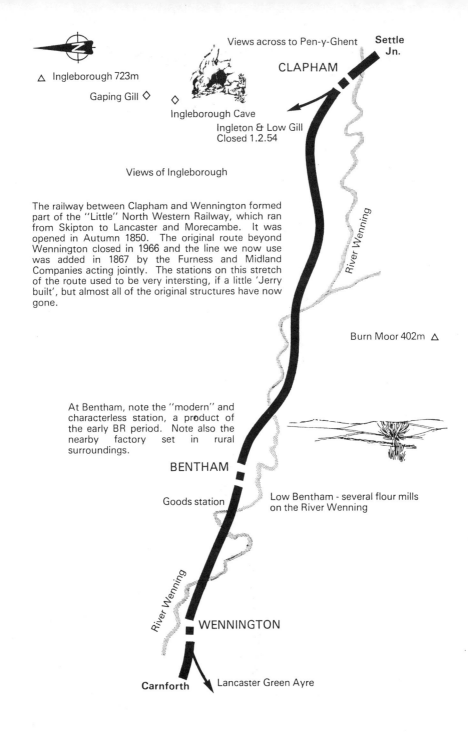

Views across to Pen-y-Ghent **Settle Jn.**

CLAPHAM

△ Ingleborough 723m

Gaping Gill ◇ ◇

Ingleborough Cave
Ingleton & Low Gill
Closed 1.2.54

Views of Ingleborough

The railway between Clapham and Wennington formed part of the "Little" North Western Railway, which ran from Skipton to Lancaster and Morecambe. It was opened in Autumn 1850. The original route beyond Wennington closed in 1966 and the line we now use was added in 1867 by the Furness and Midland Companies acting jointly. The stations on this stretch of the route used to be very intersting, if a little 'Jerry built', but almost all of the original structures have now gone.

River Wenning

Burn Moor 402m △

At Bentham, note the "modern" and characterless station, a product of the early BR period. Note also the nearby factory set in rural surroundings.

BENTHAM

Goods station

Low Bentham - several flour mills on the River Wenning

River Wenning

WENNINGTON

Carnforth ↓ Lancaster Green Ayre

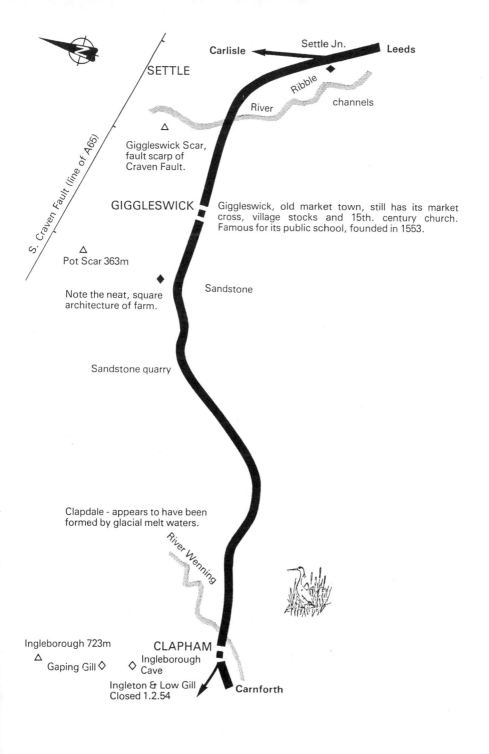

SETTLE

Carlisle ← Settle Jn. Leeds

River Ribble channels

△
Giggleswick Scar,
fault scarp of
Craven Fault.

S. Craven Fault (line of A65)

GIGGLESWICK Giggleswick, old market town, still has its market
cross, village stocks and 15th. century church.
Famous for its public school, founded in 1553.

△
Pot Scar 363m

◆
Note the neat, square
architecture of farm.

Sandstone

Sandstone quarry

Clapdale - appears to have been
formed by glacial melt waters.

River Wenning

Ingleborough 723m
△
Gaping Gill ◇   ◇ Ingleborough
Cave

CLAPHAM

Ingleton & Low Gill
Closed 1.2.54   Carnforth

SELECTED BIBLIOGRAPHY & REFERENCES

Visitor's Guides

"A Visitor's Guide to the Yorkshire Dales, Teesdale & Weardale" by Brian Spencer, published by Moorland Press.

"A Visitor's Guide to the Lake District" by Brian Spencer, published by Moorland Press.

"Skipton - Capital of Craven Mini-guide" published by Skipton Town Council.

"40 Great Attractions in West Yorkshire" published by West Yorkshire County Council.

"Howarth and the Bronte Country"

"Leeds - A Visitor's Guide" published by Leeds City Council.

"The Border City - A Young Visitor's Guide to Carlisle" published by Carlisle City Council.

"Carlisle Day Tripper" published by Carlisle City Council.

"Carlisle Town Centre Trail" published by Carlisle City Council.

"A Short History of Lancaster" published by Lancaster City Council.

Railway Books

"The Little North Western Railway" by Donald Binns, published by Wyvern Publications.

"Yorkshire Railways" by A. Haigh and David Joy, published by Dalesman Books.

"Main Line Over Shap" by David Joy, published by Dalesman Books.

"Settle to Carlisle - A Railway over the Pennines" by W. R. Mitchell and David Joy, published by Dalesman Books.

"The Scenic Settle and Carlisle Railway" by D. Binns, published by Wyvern Publications.

"Life on the Settle-Carlisle Railway" by W. R. Mitchell, published by Dalesman Books.

"Settle-Carlisle in Colour" by David Joy, published by Dalesman Books.

Maps

The route is covered by numerous maps of the Landranger, 1:50 000 scale, with some parts covered by tourist maps. Any visitor staying in the area will find such maps an invaluable aid in interpreting the countryside as well as a navigational aid.

The whole route from just north of Skipton is covered by the 1:250 000 geological map "Lake District" sheet 54N 04W. This is a valuable adjunct to the present publication, as the geology often defines what there is to see.

This is just a selection of the many books, booklets and leaflets which cover aspects of the area. Many of the leaflets are free or cost just a few pence and are usually available from tourist offices.